101 Ba... Reading for Guitar

Six Strings Music Publishing
Los Angeles, CA U.S.A.

Published by
Six Strings Music Publishing
P.O. Box 7718, Torrance, CA 90504-9118
Tel: 800-784-0203
Fax: 310-324-8544
contact@sixstringsmusicpub.com
http://www.sixstringsmusicpub.com

ISBN#: 1-891370-06-5

Copyright ©2000 by SIX STRINGS MUSIC PUBLISHING
International Copyright Secured   All Rights Reserved

The music, text, design and graphics in this publication are protected by copyright law. Any duplication or transmission, by any means, electronic, mechanical, photocopying, or otherwise, is an infringement of copyright.

Table of Contents

The Equipment You'll Need --------------------- 4

How To Hold Your Guitar ----------------------- 4

Holding A Pick -------------------------------- 4

Introduction ---------------------------------- 5

Learning Some Basics -------------------------- 6

    Guitar Parts ------------------------------ 6

    Tuning the Guitar -------------------------- 7

    Basic Music Notation ---------------------- 8

    Count (Rhythm) ---------------------------- 8

    Notes ------------------------------------- 9

    Rests ------------------------------------- 9

    Pitches and Treble Clef ------------------- 10

    Time Signature ---------------------------- 10

Reading Notes --------------------------------- 11

    Diagram & Finger Numbers ------------ 11

    Notes on the 1st String ------------------- 12

    Notes on the 2nd String ------------------- 16

    Notes on the 3rd String ------------------- 20

    Notes on the 4th String ------------------- 24

    Notes on the 5th String ------------------- 28

    Notes on the 6th String ------------------- 32

Review -- 36

Questionnaire

Order form

The Equipment You'll Need

Guitar   **Metronome**   **Pick**

How to Hold Your Guitar

Hold the guitar in whatever position is most comfortable and easiest for you. As a reference, some models in sitting positions are shown below:

Holding A Pick

There are a number of ways to hold a pick. As a reference, the most common way of holding a pick is shown here:

Introduction

Welcome to *101 Basic Reading for Guitar*. Would you like to be able to walk into any music shop, look at a piece of sheet music and work out how to play the melody without ever having heard it before? If so, then *101 Basic Reading for Guitar* is for you!

101 Basic Reading for Guitar will encourage and instruct you step by step if you are an eager beginner with your first guitar. It also can open up a new dimension if you have been playing without knowing how to read music. Being able to read music can reward you in many ways. For example, you can exchange your musical ideas with your friend or your band easily and accurately. Knowing how to read music can enhance your understanding of music theory. Most of all, reading music is fun.

In Section One, "Learning Some Basics," you will find out about guitar parts, how to tune your guitar, and basic music notation. Then, in Section Two, "Reading Notes," you will learn how to play two or three notes per string and a few rhythms step by step. An easy-to-follow diagram will guide you quickly and effectively where and how to play notes on your guitar. Warm-up exercises will accustom your fingers to play. Note-reading exercises and a brief review of new rhythms come next. Finally, a selection of easy-to-play melodies and songs will speed you along your way to a new level of enjoyment.

Here are some suggestions to use this book effectively:

- Always use a metronome.
- When learning new notes, play VERY SLOWLY at first.
- Visualize each note *before* actually playing it.
- When reading songs, always complete the piece, then go back and analyze your mistake. Don't stop or look back at a place you misplayed.
- Review regularly.

Good luck and have fun reading!

LEARNING SOME BASICS

GUITAR PARTS

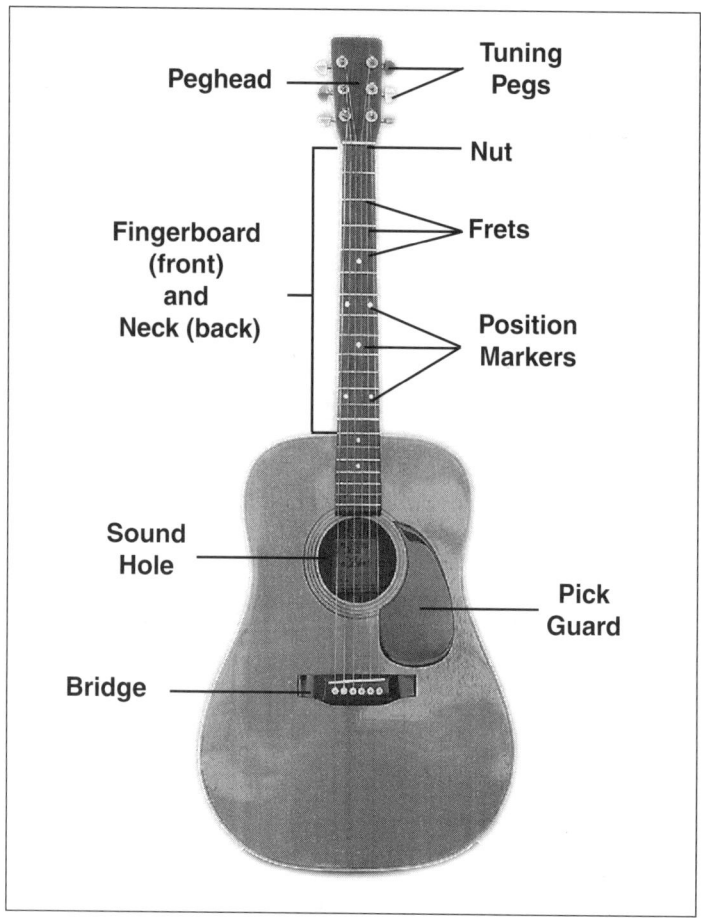

TUNING THE GUITAR

Each string of your guitar is to be tuned with a specific pitch as shown below on a piano:

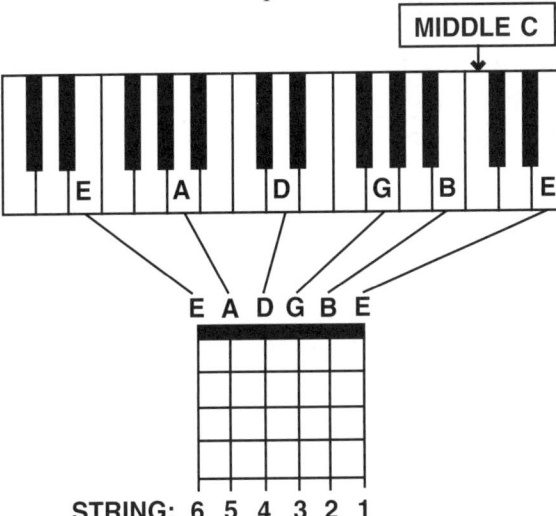

If you don't have a piano or keyboard at hand, here is another tuning method:

1. Using either a tuning fork or electric metronome which has A4 440Hz tuning pitch, tune the 5th string to A.

2. Next, press the 5th fret of the 6th string and tune it to match the open 5th string. (Open means you do not press the string.)

3. Similarly, press the 5th fret of the 5th string and tune the open 4th string to match the pitch.

4. Press the 5th fret of the 4th string and tune the open 3rd string to match it.

5. Press the 4th fret of the 3rd string and tune the open 2nd string to match it.

6. Finally, press the 5th fret of the 2nd string and tune the open 1st string to match it.

BASIC MUSIC NOTATION

Music is written on a **staff** which consists of five lines and four spaces. The staff is divided into **measures** or **bars**. A **bar line** separates one measure from another. A **double bar line** indicates the end of a piece of music. **Repeat signs** tell you that the music between the signs is to be played once more.

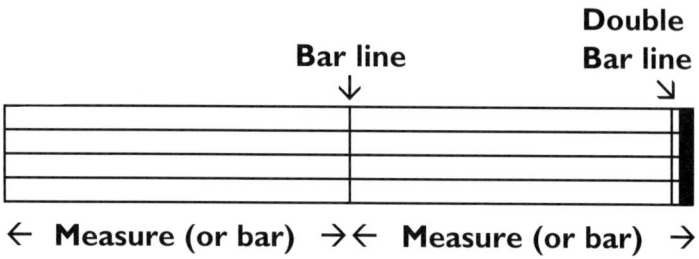

COUNT (RHYTHM)

Music is played with a definite beat or rhythm. It is a steady and regular pulse or **count** throughout the music similar to the ticking of a clock. To see how regular a count is, turn on your metronome and pace yourself with each click while tapping your foot and counting ONE-TWO-THREE-FOUR, ONE-TWO-THREE-FOUR, etc. Whenever you read or play music, always follow each click carefully and make sure you are playing *in time* without dragging or rushing.

NOTES

Notes are symbols that indicate musical sounds. How many counts or how long you sustain or hold the sound depends on what kind of notes you are playing.

NOTES	NAME	COUNTS
𝅝	Whole note	Played and sustained for **4 counts**
𝅗𝅥	Half note	Played and sustained for **2 counts**
𝅘𝅥	Quarter note	Played and sustained for **1 count**
𝅘𝅥𝅮	Eighth note	Played and sustained for **1/2 count**
𝅗𝅥.	Dotted half note	Played and sustained for **3 counts**
𝅘𝅥.	Dotted quarter note	Played and sustained for **1 & 1/2 counts**

RESTS

Rests indicate silence. How many counts or how long you *don't* play depends on what kind of rest symbols you have.

RESTS	NAME	COUNTS TO REST
𝄻	Whole rest	Rest for **4 counts**
𝄼	Half rest	Rest for **2 counts**
𝄽	Quarter rest	Rest for **1 count**
𝄾	Eighth rest	Rest for **1/2 count**

PITCHES AND TREBLE CLEF

A **pitch** tells us how low or high the sound of the note is. It is indicated by where you find a note on the staff. Pitches are named alphabetically using the seven English letters A, B, C, D, E, F, and G. After G, we begin again with A. The **treble clef** placed at the beginning of a piece of music indicates that any note placed on the 2nd line from the bottom will be called a G. The other notes will be named alphabetically based on this reference point.

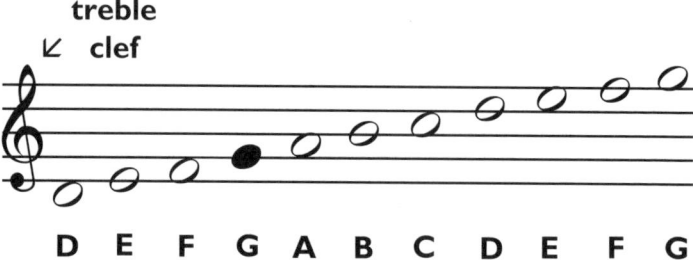

TIME SIGNATURE

Time Signature is placed at the beginning of every song next to the treble clef. It shows you both how many counts there are in each measure and what kind of note will represent one count or beat.

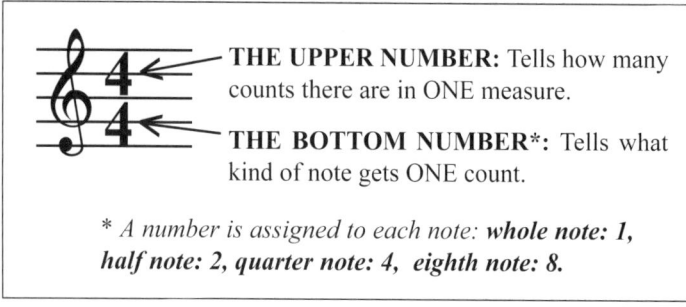

e.g. **4/4:** 4 counts in a measure & the quarter note gets 1 count.
3/4: 3 counts in a measure & the quarter note gets 1 count.

READING NOTES

DIAGRAM & FINGER NUMBERS

A diagram shows a portion of the guitar fingerboard. Six vertical lines represent strings, from left to right, 6th, 5th, 4th, 3rd, 2nd, and 1st. Horizontal lines represent frets. The thick horizontal line at the very top is the nut.

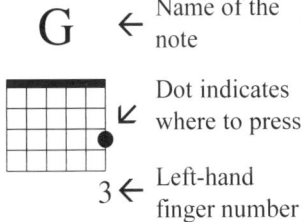

- G ← Name of the note
- Dot indicates where to press
- 3 ← Left-hand finger number

Left-hand finger numbers:
- **T**: Thumb
- **1**: 1st finger
- **2**: 2nd finger
- **3**: 3rd finger
- **4**: 4th finger

TAB

A tablature or TAB is a six-line staff graphically showing the fingerboard. Each of the six lines represents one of the guitar strings as shown below. The numbers that appear on the lines are fret numbers indicating where to press down. "0" means open string, "2" means the 2nd fret, etc.

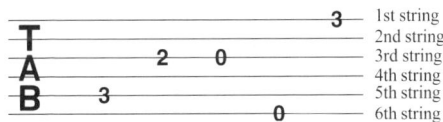

NOTES ON THE 1ST STRING

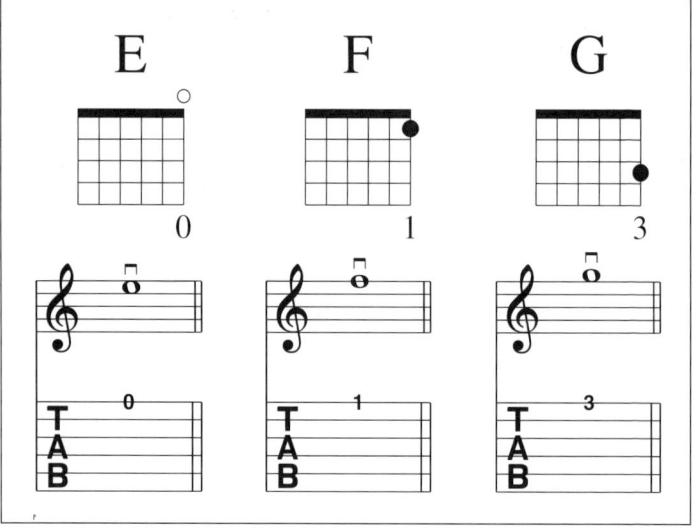

Let's first learn three notes **E, F,** and **G** on the 1st string. As shown above, the open 1st string without fingering will produce E. F can be played by pressing the 1st fret with your 1st finger. Press the 3rd fret with your 3rd finger, and you'll get G. The symbol, ⊓ , indicates a **downstroke.** Strike the string downward toward the floor.

Practice these three notes with the warm-up exercises on the next page. Play very SLOWLY at first and make sure you play each note cleanly and strongly without any buzz. After you're comfortable playing the notes, set a metronome to 44~46 and synchronize with each click.

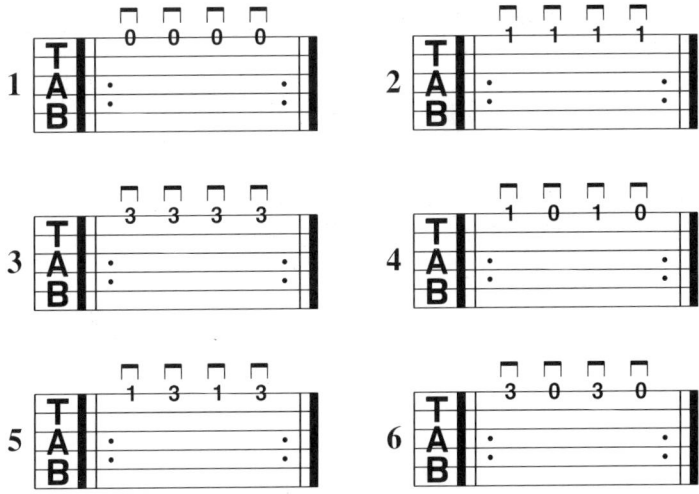

Let's practice reading notes without TAB. Play and sustain a note for four clicks first, next for two clicks, and finally for every click of your metronome. Visualize each note, and play it through. Read backwards. Read every other line, and increase the tempo.

WHOLE NOTE AND WHOLE REST

Now, we add rhythm. In this section, we read whole notes and whole rests only. If you recall, a whole note gets **four counts**: Play a note on count *1* and sustain it for four counts (*1-2-3-4*) to complete a measure. At a whole rest, *do not* play for four counts. Place your right-hand palm on the strings and stop the sound completely.

First Song

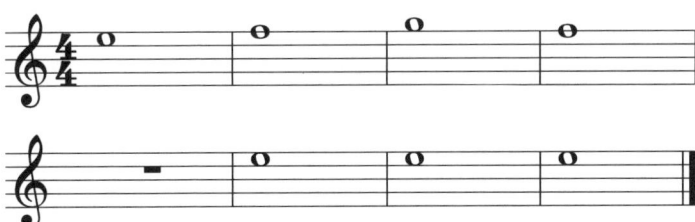

Holes

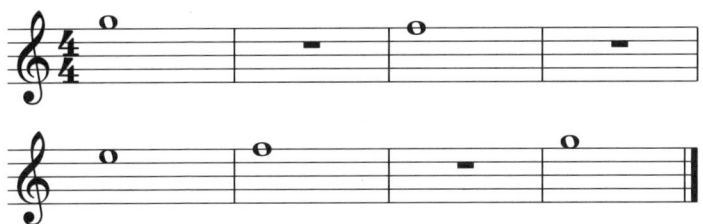

Wholeheartedly

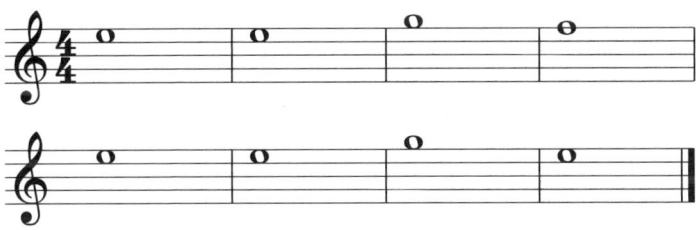

Isn't It Fun?

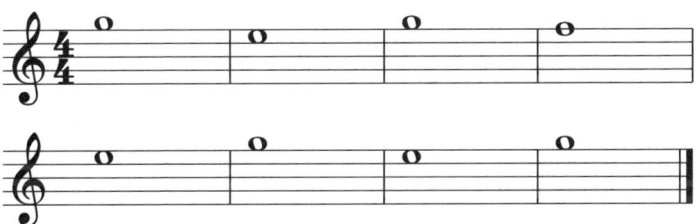

NOTES ON THE 2ND STRING

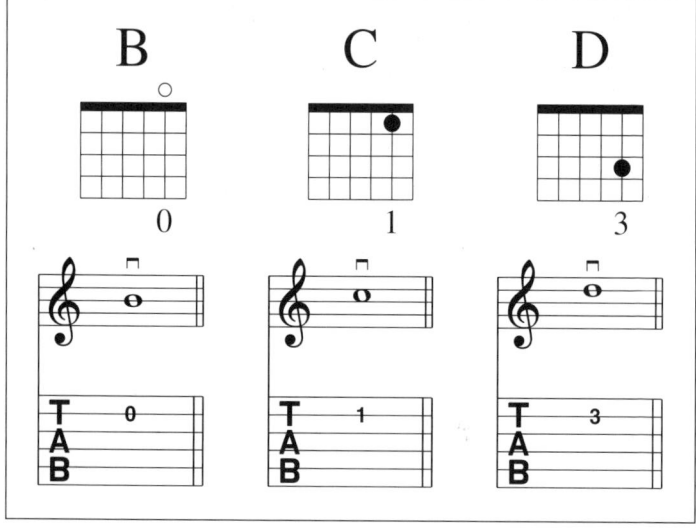

The notes to learn on the 2nd string are **B, C,** and **D**. The B note is the same as the open 2nd string. C can be played by pressing the 1st fret with your 1st finger. Press the 3rd fret with your 3rd finger, and you'll have D. Use all downstrokes.

Practice these three notes with the warm-up exercises on the next page. Play very SLOWLY at first and make sure you play each note cleanly and strongly without any buzz. Set a metronome to 44~46 and strive to synchronize with each click. Notice in the last three exercises, you'll be moving from string to string. Practice the transition *very* slowly.

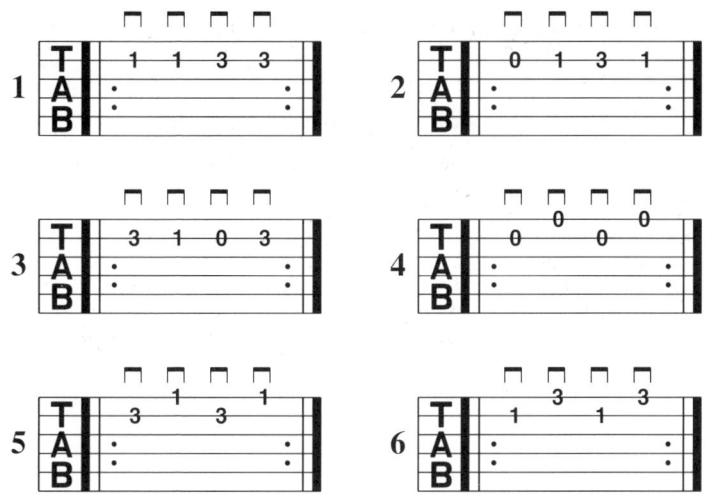

Let's practice reading notes without TAB. Play and sustain a note for four clicks first, next for two clicks, and finally for every click of your metronome. Visualize each note, and play it through. Read backwards. Read every other line, and increase the tempo.

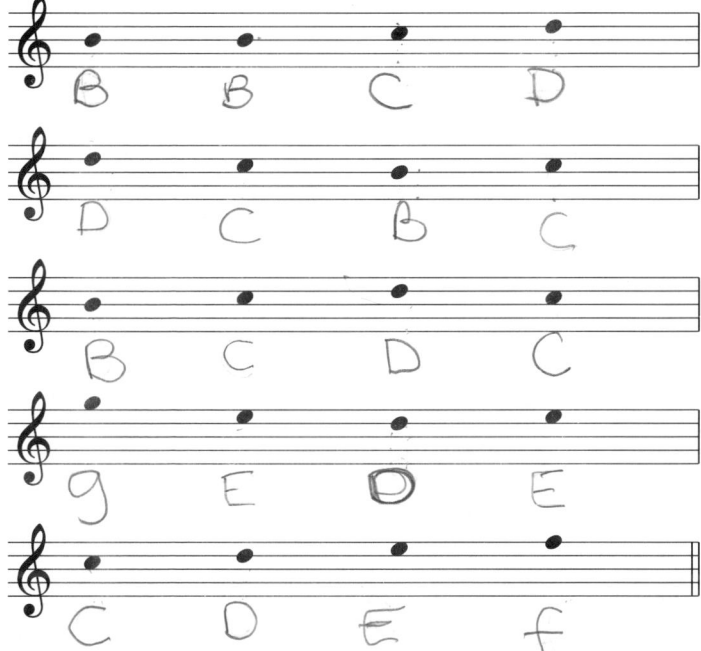

HALF NOTE AND HALF REST

Now, let's add two new rhythms: half-notes and half rests. To review, a half note gets **two counts**. Play a note on count *1* or *3* and sustain it for two counts. There can be two half notes in a measure. When you see a half rest, rest for two counts. Make sure to mute the sound completely by placing your right-hand palm on the strings.

19

First Half

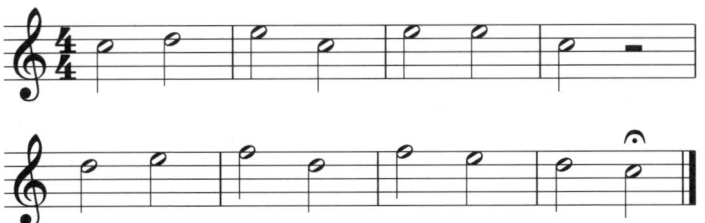

◠ is called **Fermata**, and it indicates that the note is to be held slightly longer.

Half N Half

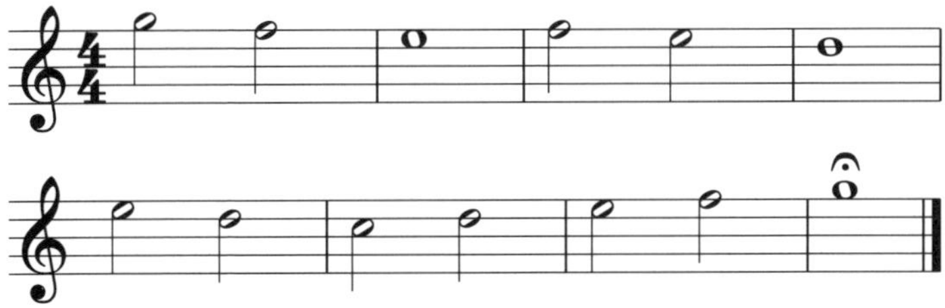

Ode To Joy

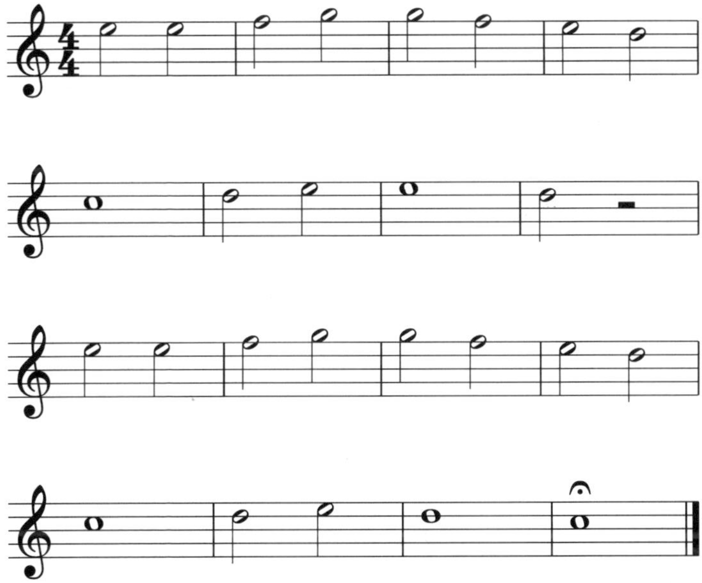

NOTES ON THE 3RD STRING

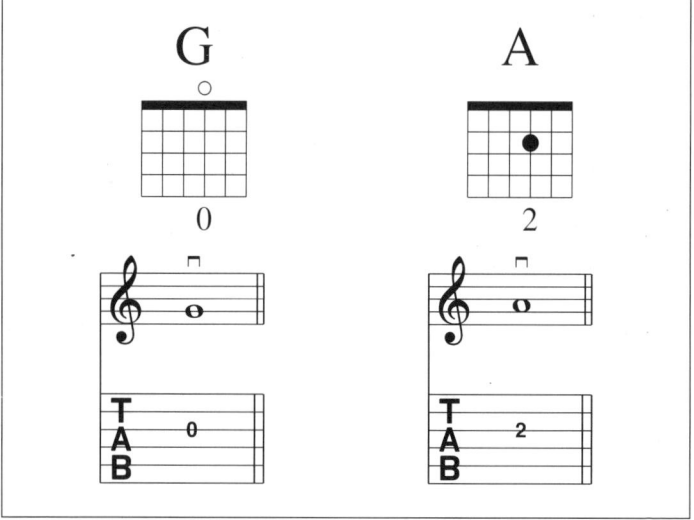

The two notes we are going to learn on the 3rd string are **G** and **A**. Play the open 3rd string as shown above, and you'll get G. A can be played by pressing the 2nd fret with your 2nd finger. As before, use all downstrokes.

Practice these two notes with the warm-up exercises on the next page. Play very SLOWLY at first and play each note cleanly and strongly without any buzz. Set a metronome to 44~46 and strive to synchronize with each click. In some of the exercises, you'll be moving from string to string. Keep practicing the transition slowly until you can do it without looking at the guitar.

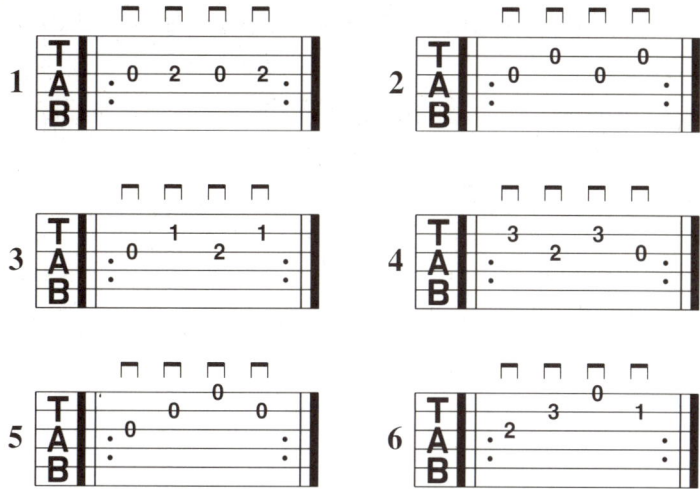

Let's practice reading notes without TAB. Play and sustain a note for four clicks first, next for two clicks, and finally for every click of your metronome. Visualize each note, and play it through. Read backwards. Read every other line, and increase the tempo.

QUARTER NOTE AND QUARTER REST

Let's add two new rhythms: the quarter note and quarter rest. A quarter note gets **one count**: Play a note on each count. There can be four quarter notes in a measure. When you see a quarter rest, you will be silent for one count. As before, place your right-hand palm on the strings and shut out the sound completely at any rest symbols.

Jingle Bells

***rit.** is called **Ritardando**, and it means to slow down gradually.

Aura Lee

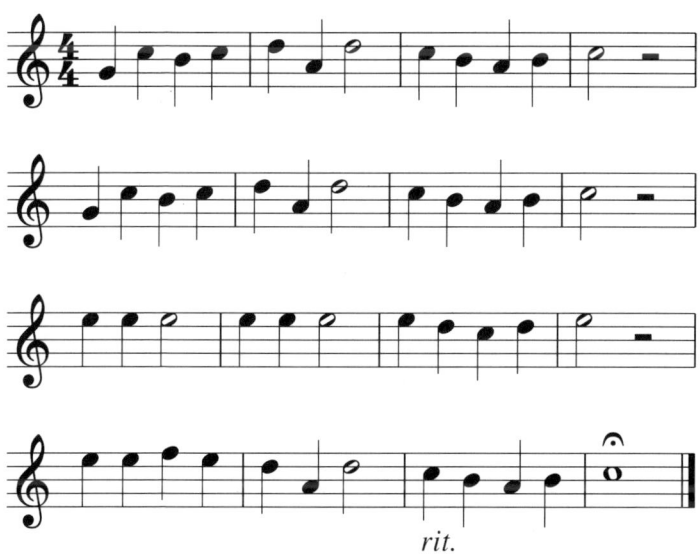

NOTES ON THE 4TH STRING

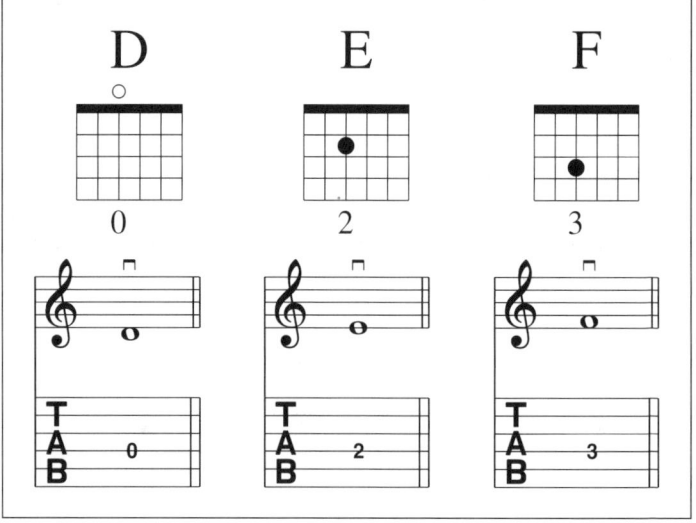

The notes on the 4th string we are going to learn are **D, E,** and **F**. The open 4th string is note D. Press the 2nd fret with your 2nd finger, and you'll get E. F is on the 3rd fret. Press it with your 3rd finger. Pick each note with downstrokes.

Warm yourself up with the exercises on the next page. Play very SLOWLY at first and make sure you play each note cleanly and strongly without any buzz. Set a metronome at a comfortable tempo at first and strive to synchronize with each click. Practice the movement between consecutive strings slowly until you can do it without looking at the guitar.

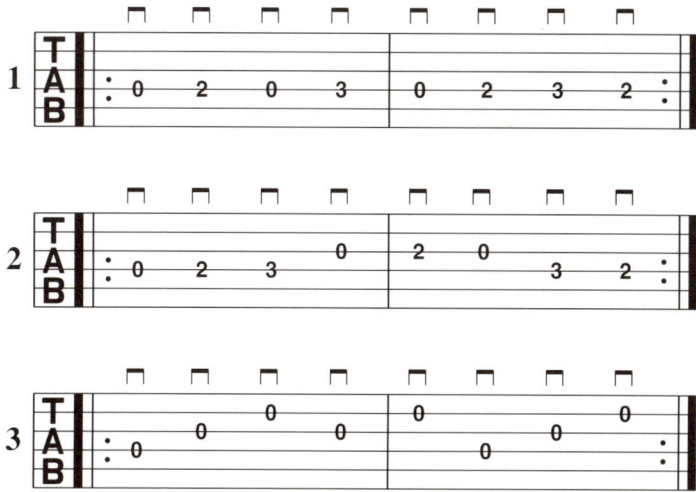

Let's practice reading notes without TAB. Play and sustain a note for four clicks first, next for two clicks, and finally for every click of your metronome. Visualize each note, and play it through. Read backwards. Read every other line, and increase the tempo.

DOTTED HALF NOTE AND TIE

A dot next to a note increases its note value by half. So, a dotted half note gets **three counts** while a dotted quarter note is held for **one and half counts.**

A curved line (⌣) connecting two notes of the same pitch is called a **tie**. Play the first note and sustain it for the time value of both notes combined. In the example below, a quarter note, F, is connected with a tie to another F quarter note. In this case, you play the first F and hold it for two counts. Do not attack the second F note.

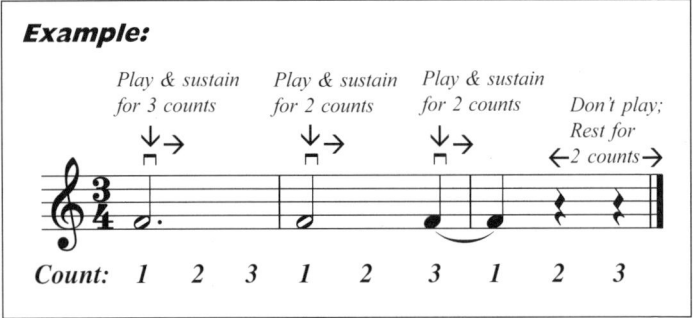

3/4

Notice the new time signature, 3/4 in the example and the songs on the next page. To review, in 3/4, there are **three beats** in a measure and **a quarter note gets one count.** The only difference between 4/4 and 3/4 is the number of counts in a measure. The rest is the same.

Pick-Up Notes

As you can see on the next page, not all music begins on beat one. Notes before the first full measure (before the double bar line) are called **pick-up notes**. Count off as usual and play the first note at the appropriate count as shown.

In The Good Old Summer Time

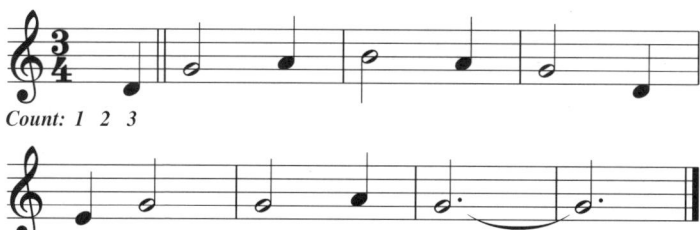

Down In The Valley

Oh, Susanna

NOTES ON THE 5TH STRING

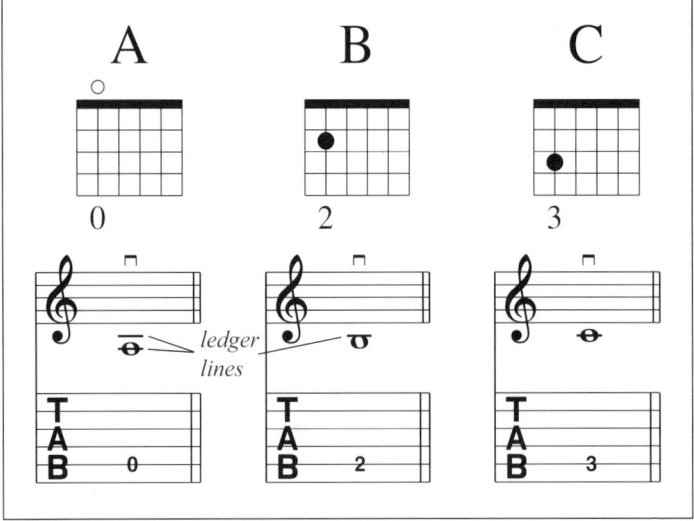

On the 5th string, we have three notes: **A, B,** and **C**. Short lines where notes are placed are called *ledger lines*. They are used for notes too high or too low in pitch to fit on the staff.

Notice in the warm-up exercises on the next page, we have a new picking symbol, ∨. This symbol indicates an **upstroke.** Pick a note from the floor toward the ceiling. As shown in the exercises, practice alternating downstrokes and upstrokes. Play very SLOWLY at first and make sure you play each note cleanly and evenly. Set a metronome to a slow tempo first and strive to synchronize with each click.

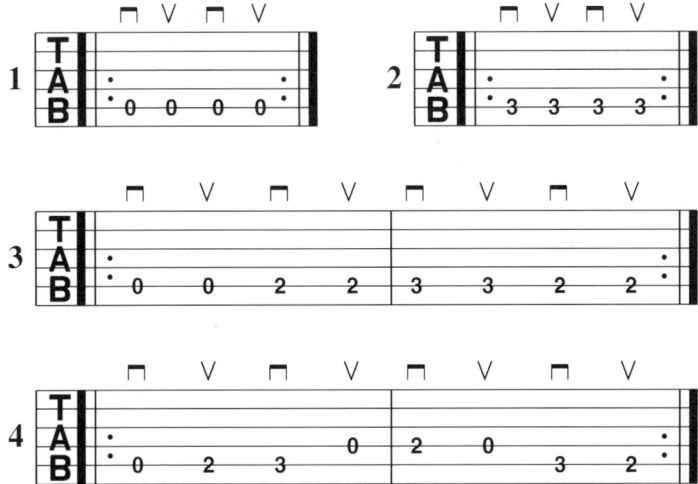

Let's practice reading notes without TAB. Play and sustain a note for four clicks first, next for two clicks, and finally for every click of your metronome. Visualize each note, and play it through. Read backwards. Read every other line, and increase the tempo.

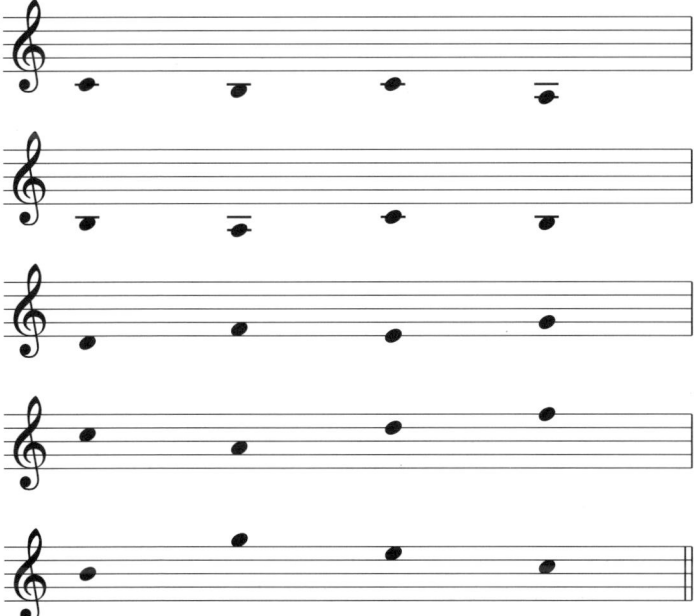

EIGHTH NOTE AND EIGHTH REST

Now, let's learn new rhythms: the eighth note and eighth rest. To review, an eighth note gets **one-half count.** There are two eighth notes in one count. To get a feel for an eighth note, think of dividing a quarter note or each click of your metronome exactly by half, and count **1-&-2-&-3-&-4-&.** Alternate downstrokes and upstrokes evenly; downstrokes on the counts *1, 2, 3, 4* and upstrokes on every "*&.*" Practice very *slowly* until you feel comfortable with the counting and down and up picking. An eighth rest gets a rest for one-half count.

BEAM

When you have a group of two or more eighth notes, they are usually connected by a thin, horizontal line, called a **beam.**

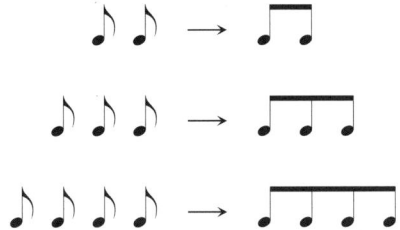

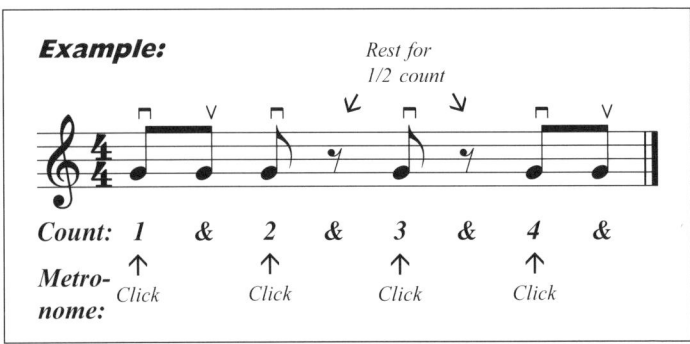

On Top of Old Smokey

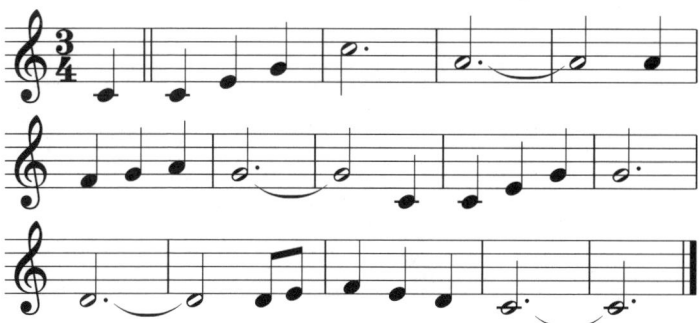

Amazing Grace

When The Saints Go Marching In

NOTES ON THE 6TH STRING

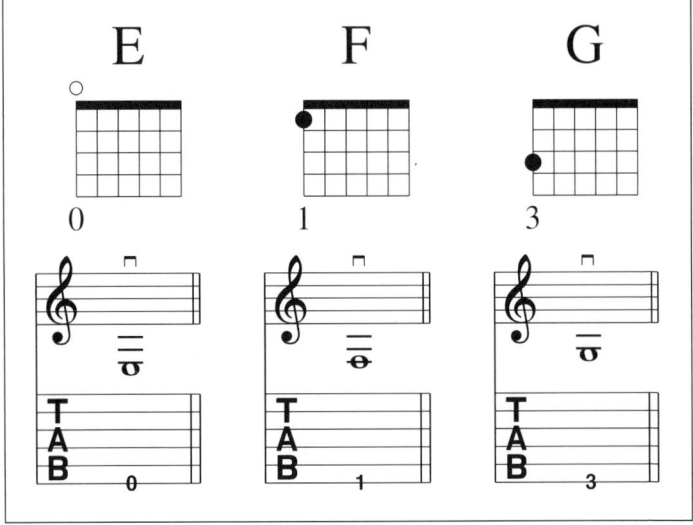

There are three notes to learn on the 6th string: **E, F,** and **G**. The E note is the same as open 6th string. F can be played by pressing the 1st fret with your 1st finger. Press the 3rd fret with your 3rd finger, and you'll have G.

Practice these three notes with the warm-up exercises on the next page. As in the 5th string section, alternate downstrokes and upstrokes. Play very SLOWLY at first and make sure you play each note cleanly and evenly. Strive to synchronize with each click of your metronome. Practice moving from one string to another slowly until you can do it without looking at the guitar.

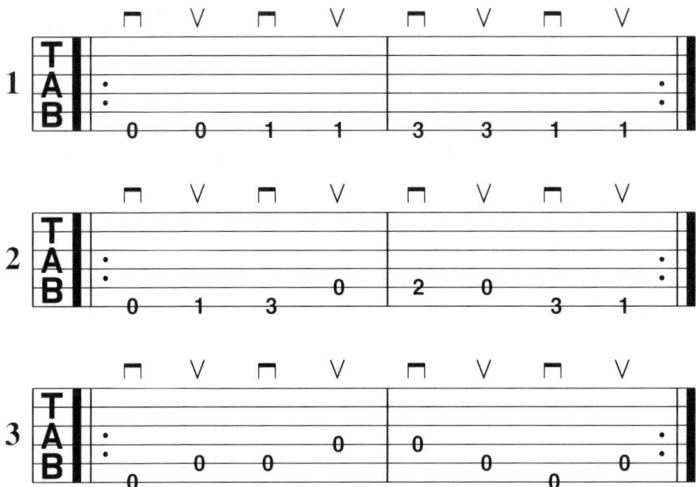

Let's practice reading notes without TAB. Play and sustain a note for four clicks first, next for two clicks, and finally for every click of your metronome. Visualize each note, and play it through. Read backwards. Read every other line, and increase the tempo.

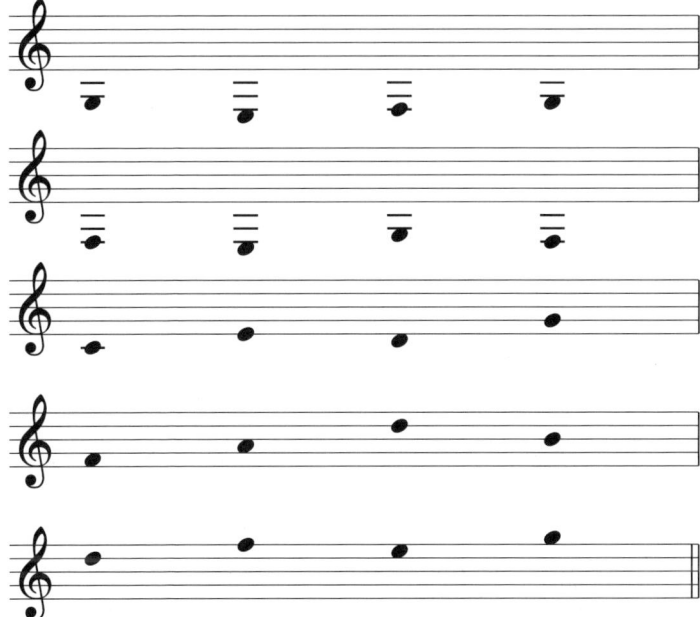

DOTTED QUARTER NOTE

Now, let's add a new rhythm: the dotted quarter note. If you recall, a dot next to a note increases its note value by half (see p. 26). So, a dotted quarter note is held for **one and half counts.**

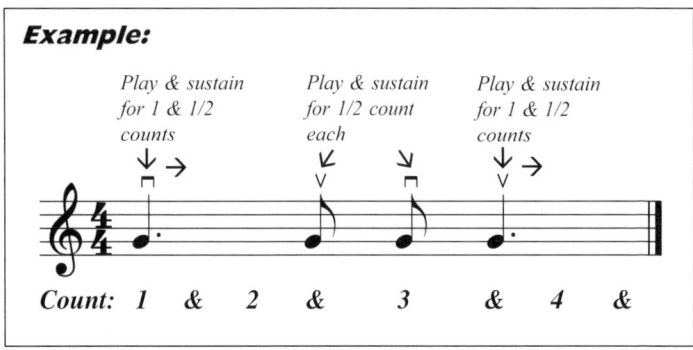

TEMPO MARKINGS

Tempo or how fast or slow music is to be played is indicated either by a metronomic setting or by an Italian or English descriptive term. Below are some of the musical terms with approximate metronome markings. Take out your metronome to identify the tempo that each term defines.

ITALIAN TERMS	ENGLISH TERMS	METRO-NOME
Largo	Very Slowly	40-60
Larghetto (Lento)	Slowly	60-66
Adagio	Slowly at ease	66-76
Andante	Moderately (walking speed)	76-108
Moderato	Moderately	108-120
Allegro	Fast	120-168
Presto	Very Fast	168-200

Peace Like A River

Just As I Am

REVIEW

Good Night, Ladies
Moderately

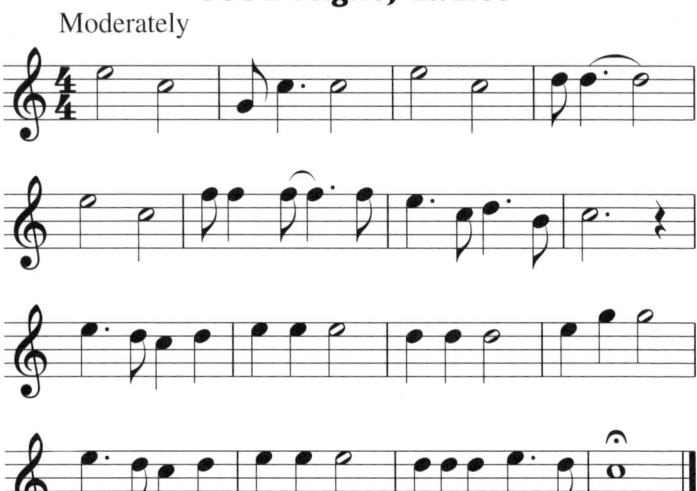

Oh My Darling Clementine
Adagio

Old Folks At Home

Slowly

rit.

Red Wing

Moderately

ALSO AVAILABLE FROM SIX STRINGS MUSIC PUBLISHING

101 Basic **Guitar Chords**
022 .... $6.95

101 Basic **Minor Pentatonic Scales**
030 .... $6.95

101 Basic **Major Pentatonic Scales**
049 .... $6.95

101 Basic **Blues Scales**
057 .... $6.95

101 Basic **Reading for Guitar**
065 .... $6.95

Guitar Chords and Accompaniment
006 .... $14.95

***More* Guitar Chords and Accompaniment**
014 .... $14.95

QUESTIONNAIRE

Thank you for your purchase of *101 Basic Reading for Guitar.* Your suggestions, questions and comments would be greatly appreciated. Please take the time to fill out this questionnaire and send it to: **Six Strings Music Publishing, P.O. Box 7718, Torrance, CA 90504.**

1. Where did you purchase this book?

2. How long have you been playing the guitar?

3. If you are a teacher, how long have you been teaching? What other books have you been using?

4. Which music magazines do you regularly read?

5. What music books or videos do you use and like?

6. What kinds of music books would you like to see in the future?

7. What is your favorite type of music? Who is your favorite musician or music group?

8. Comments or suggestions regarding this book:

ORDER FORM

Title	Qty	Unit Price	Subtotal
			$
			$
			$
			$
			$
		Subtotal	$
		Sales Tax *(CA residents, add 7.25%; LA county, add 8.25%)*	$
		Shipping	$ 4.50
		TOTAL	$

☐ **CHECK OR MONEY ORDER ENCLOSED (U.S. ONLY)**

☐ **CREDIT CARD:** ☐ Visa ☐ Master Card ☐ Amex

Card Number: _____

Name on Card: _____ **Exp. Date:** _____

Prices subject to change without notice. No C.O.D. orders.

MAILING ADDRESS

Name: _____ **Age:** _____

Address: _____

City: _____ **State:** _____ **Zip:** _____

Tel: _____

> Please place your order to Six Strings Music Publishing:
> *Mail*: P.O. Box 7718, Torrance, CA 90504-9118
> *Tel*: 800-784-0203 / *Fax*: 310-324-8544
> *E-mail*: order@sixstringsmusicpub.com
> *On-line*: http://www.sixstringsmusicpub.com